The Lama's English Lessons

Poems by Tony Trigilio

The Lama's English Lessons

winner of the **three candles press first book award**

judged by Joseph Millar

9/26/07

For Chip —

Thanks for coming to Kent!

Yeah!

three candles press

www.threecandlespress.com

For Shelly Hubman and Carmen Trigilio

Contents

IV. The Lama's English Lessons

Notes

Acknowledgments

Grateful acknowledgments to the editors of the following journals and anthologies in which some of these poems appeared, often in different versions: *America Zen: A Gathering of Poets, The Beloit Poetry Journal; Columbia Poetry Review, Digerati: 20 Contemporary Poets in the Virtual World, Eleventh Muse; Hotel Amerika; The Iowa Review; Jack, The Laurel Review, Listening Eye, New Orleans Review, Rhino, The Spoon River Poetry Review*, and *three candles journal.*

Special thanks

Jan Bottiglieri, Brenda Cárdenas, Kevin Cassell, Nina Corwin, Mitch Evich, Chris Green, Arielle Greenberg, Rick Hilles, Larry Janowski, Joseph Millar, Steve Mueske, and David Trinidad. Thanks to the Ragdale Foundation for its support. I am grateful for Michael Trigilio's gift of friendship and inspiration. Thank you, Shelly, for love, wisdom, spirit.

Interior Design: Steve Mueske
Cover Design: Michael Trigilio

Library of Congress Control Number: 2006937993

Choosing a Stone

Flat-stone perfect skipping-stone,
a book I find on the library shelf
on my way to the book I wanted
to find, the lane-change I make
without checking my rear-view mirror,
the moment I sign my credit-card receipt
and, only then, realize I bought
a burgundy ribbed sweater
because a television model wore it
on a commercial. The thing-itself,
the flat skipping stone I think I find
by accident. But it's waiting for us,
lost in plain sight — sea shells, bottle caps,
amid useless chips and stones,
their geometry fractured.
I find it in the same way I cannot coax
the cat from a dark corner of the attic.
Don't say *here, kitty*. No silly whistling,
as if she can be fooled into thinking
I've become an absent-minded robin.
She comes to me like the first time
I noticed my shadow at night,
a smudge on pavement cast by street lamp.
I sit still on the floor, the center of the attic.
Light a candle, place it beside me.
Sit still, flat as a rock.

I

Five Verses for Shariputra Mugged Outside His Building

The Longest Continuing Running Policeman

—Jack Lord, 1920–1998

The longest continuing running policeman
shows a connection to when I experienced
what felt like something entering my body
in my sleep suddenly causing me to awaken
in March of '77 — at the Hawaii Holiday Inn
whose name has just been changed
and was never part of the Holiday Inn chain
— shows a connection to the heavenly part
of this, what I felt when something entered
my body. Hawaii is the "Paradise of the Pacific."
The fact that the name of the show was *Hawaii Five-O*
shows a connection to Christ, the longest continuing
running policeman, the heavenly part of this.
He polices us all, if you please. The *O* is the circle
and it's about time it became unbroken.
The fact that Jack Lord was 77 when having heart failure
relates to the graduation process, our awakening
to be Christ. The *5* of course is Christ, the *O*
is the circle and it's about time it became unbroken.
Something entered my body in March of '77
at the Hawaii Holiday Inn whose name has been changed
and I've been trying to reclaim my heart ever since —
shows a connection to the heavenly part of this.
The headline read, "Jack Lord, Star of *Hawaii Five-O*, Dies."
The line below read in smaller type, "Producer of longest
continuously running police show suffers heart failure
at 77." In Luke 3:23 (March 23) Jesus is 77th in the line of God —
connects to both me and Jesus in a genealogy of Jesus.
As Christ, I am born with heart failure, what felt like
something entering my body in sleep causing me to awaken.

The 5 of course is Christ. *Jack* is J-A-C-K, or JA.
It's about time it became unbroken, the *O* is the circle.
Jack is also 1132 (Jesus is 11 and Christ 32), which is a 7,
or Jesus Christ reduced. The 5 of course is Christ.
The fact that the name of the show was *Hawaii Five-O*
shows a connection to Christ and the heavenly part.
Jesus Christ is *Lord*. Hawaii is the Paradise.
Don't you think it's time you put me to work for you?
Or do you just want me to continue to be around
in merely a mediocre existence in fact?
Something entered my body March 23, 1977,
at the Hawaii Holiday Inn whose name has been changed
and I've been trying to reclaim my heart ever since —
shows a connection to the heavenly part of this.
As Christ, I am born with heart failure, causing me to awaken.

Jack Lord is a Tough Professional

He has a whole collection of poetry and prose he has saved over a lifetime.
                                    —TV GUIDE profile, 1971

I had no idea what the energy was composed of, when a being identified as Lord appeared to me when I was living in Little Rock.

Tempered in the crucible of the New York stage, a highly disciplined product of the theater, steeped in the art of acting.

I was called to the island then. I was 26 when I was re-awakened.
Jack Lord appeared. It was 1968. I knew I'd never leave the islands.

He is no laconic, virginal cowboy.

The lady I was staying with offered me a free trip to Kauai for my birthday and a free session with an astrologer. I told her I'm just a numerologist

and I wouldn't need my TV anymore. Listening is a way of becoming. After Oahu, I realized I wasn't there for the conference.

Here he is not the actor playing to an audience of one. He is sharing.

All energy centers are identifiable. From the sacral centers on Big Island to the crown above Iolani Palace. When I went to work here, I told Lord

I was a Kauai Emissary calling Omaha to this place.

Once I remembered I'd lived here many lifetimes ago in a damp cave, he began an inner dialogue with me.

He wanted to be a motion-picture actor but he's a pragmatist, a tough professional.

Every morning he tells me, "The real victory's survival, babe, Buffalo Bill's defunct."
I am in cellular remembrance of this place, with great love respect and aloha.

He reads me St. Vincent Millay, "singing sweet songs to please himself."

He possesses a striking facial bone structure for which cameras have an affinity.

Five Verses for Shariputra Mugged Outside His Building

1.
Just a few car lengths from his front door
an old man stepped in Shariputra's way,
flat head curled, his pool-shark cap,
eyes gaping yellow and streaked with sizzled wires.
You'd think he didn't know Shariputra
just stepped out to mail a letter, actually a poem
to a woman he exchanged business cards with
on the train last week. She is broke,
dying a little with her savings every day.
In the poem Shariputra climbs
Mount Monadnock and looks across
tops of trees and sun setting
on New Hampshire and honestly believes
he cannot fall. "When I take a breath," he tells her,
"I am sure I will exhale. Why do I live each day
like I did on that mountain,
singularly sure I will not fall, though
evidence shows me the body is fragile,
docile, its perfect accomplishment dying?"

2.
Just these car lengths from home
the pool-shark man stepped in his way
and Shariputra walked around him.
Another man a block away yelled something
when Shariputra dropped the envelope
in the mailbox. Shariputra made a note:
this box is not picked up till four tomorrow.
He saw the shark-cap man with a woman
now laughing at the other man a block away

now running — and Shariputra regretted all this,
since he could wake early to mail this
tomorrow. Brighton Center's post office
picks up by nine in the morning.

3.
Now two car lengths from the mailbox
four college students who live above him
parallel parked their car and Shariputra
heard running increase behind him.
The man who was shouting kicked
Shariputra's feet, but he has vowed himself
an altruistic mind and managed not to fall.
The man was yelling and Shariputra
could not understand him, the words came
too fast, not even Sanskrit could save them.
The moon watched like a polished stone —
and as the man hit his face,
Shariputra knew the moonstone came
from underwater and his neighbors
probably were afraid to get out of their car.
Give me what you've got. Give me the wallet.
Shariputra handed it to him but touched it
first to his forehead — almost cost him his life.
The man snatched it from him too late:
Shariputra already blessed it, praying
credit cards could bring
this man good health, even bliss.

4.
But Shariputra lost his glasses, and this really is why the moon
took on its underwater luster. His cheek stung and something
swelled his face — with each heartbeat more swelling.

5.
Just a few car lengths from home,
his neighbors parallel parking,
and Shariputra thought he might die.
He could not see the man's lips move:

10

You got nothing here. No cash. Give me the cash
right now or you're a dead man.
But Shariputra had nothing, his glasses
were only made from plastic and he could not think
of anything else except his apartment keys.
He has no self and he said take this body —
you are so angry only this body can help.
The man kicked him to the ground and then
a few more times.
Shariputra gave up his vows then, saying
sentient beings are numberless and I
cannot help them because I never will know
what they want — their desire is a mystery.
I think I am bleeding.
What are you going to do about it?
Shariputra got up, began walking away,
expected a knife in his back.
"Not a thing. No thing. I don't know."

Lawyers for the Animals

She was folding clothes, always, Ada the table-dancer from New Orleans, her age grows on her like ivy and she works double-shifts when someone calls in sick, folds neighborhood clothes behind her six-inch black-and-white TV. She spent the night in the laundromat in a blizzard last year, an entire city of cabs nuzzled in warm garages, bottle of Amaretto and a couch braced and double-locked against the door. Now after two straight days of rain she stacked clothes in front of her, as if fastening a chain of paper clips together on the last day of an office job — maybe no going-away party, nothing left to mark time but someone else's paper clips. She tells me that she's doing whole wardrobes these days, there's so much flooding. I tell her ducks are swimming in the park. If she won the lottery, she would buy the Cambridge Ramada Inn and convert it into a hotel for animals. She would hire veterinarians to check on them daily, caretakers to feed them. The hotel belongs to animals. She told me, look, we got lawyers for everybody but not for the animals. They got rights, too. Last year, some girl in Quincy got bit by a Doberman. What do they do? They said they gotta kill the Doberman. But who's gonna stick up for the animals? How do we know that girl wasn't teasing the dog? That's why we need lawyers. The next day, Ada's ducks, an armada, sailed plots of grass where we stood last week straight as bankers parceling them bread crumbs. My downstairs neighbor paddled his girlfriend to work bobbing in their rubber raft, a dog swimming beside them, snout pointed to the sky.

In the Intersection, Jackson and State

Without looking, I could cross Jackson
without getting struck, guided by voices, a hum
of tires on coarse pavement. I want to scale
one of those slopes, the blushed steel
of the CNA Building, grab the Monadnock's
frayed terra cotta drapery and climb.

Lakeside wind so loud it changes the subject.
In dreams, I lie too long on spring grass, pikes
still dead despite thaw. Ants crawl my arms,
bees swarm. Nature an antique, an abandoned
oak table behind glass, waiting for me
to test its legs, barter a price.

I'm afraid of nature. Orange, Brown Line
trains cross paths, the distant touch of negotiators.
Rivers changing course, office windows bound in mist.
Pavement accumulates, dismantles, rises; an array of noise
come again. One block east, a construction crew
is drilling, their hammers lift from State like smoke.

Grace Notes

So we lived / And chose to live / These were our times.
— George Oppen

1.
Music is rustled out of dialect. You know the pavement
by accent, soft vowel Cambridge confident enough

to hang around a couple extra beats. North End stings —
take a whiff of the docks, the tang. Mouths scratch in alleys,

condo owners hush their dogs. Music is rustled
out of language, a dialect with an army and navy.

You read it somewhere, tell yourself it's true:
a musician's someone too broke to buy records.

2.
Soundchecks rumble at sundown in Allston;
listen to your voice in a mirror, face-down, peaking.

Half-songs in distortion for tired men gone deaf
twiddling sound boards — they know a few things very well.

When it's done, you leave microphone nests, lean-to
guitar stands. This is our time, you remind yourself,

the bar nuzzled at happy-hour, strained by light.
Wine glasses upside down, bats in their fulsome rattle.

3.
A few blocks down Harvard Ave., wet broccoli swells.
Swallow each bite before you let yourself take another.

Friends ask nothing of the poets among them,
minimalists of the imagination.

Our songs are grace notes for the future, they double back
like whistling snow if we're lucky. We sit down, this meal

lasts till we go on, midnight. Our soundman sniffs
in perfect contempt at the edge of the garden

of the genuine, these times we choose to live.

Swinging Man

He's come wasted, hungry,
Jackson platform
commuter outpatients
dropping coins.
Chicago swings all night,
Division Street empties
like a cat just out

of the box,
ears prickly turrets.

Each sound still
learning to glide,
what's stretched to us
feels tight to him.
His violin
attracts the sound
of friends, notes that

depart now.
Silence should be
newsworthy
between trains.

Summer is another comedy,
this clear morning
thorny, more warm

than it really needs
to be. Above us,
first and last days,
end times. For once,

you can feel.
Old men shirtless
rearrange flowerpots
on windowsills.
I smell the lake
this summer, although
everything turns to oxide
and the subway

has its own sense
of smell, enters

you like meter
when you descend
the stairs.

Holds its breath.
An old man
touched himself today

a musician studying for
your last dollar bill.

His collar, scarf
secret thermal pants
tucked away —
a warm subject unfolded
in liner notes.

Ball Game on the Car Radio

Whenever I can, I always watch the Detroit Tigers on the radio.
—Gerald Ford

Although the ball game is hard to watch on the radio,
if we could swing and keep swinging,
as the traffic backs up,
the hot bats, the heavy lumber,

we could swing and keep swinging
through clotted toll booths, open up a few lanes,
the hot bats, the heavy lumber,
even though we don't believe enough to follow anyone

through clotted toll booths. Open up a few lanes,
your throat clearing till everyone shuts up —
although we don't believe enough to follow anyone,
they know you have something to say.

Your throat clearing till everyone shuts up,
lovers so sorry for their hot words, their swinging.
They know you have something to say,
that you're sitting on a fastball.

Lovers so sorry for their hot words, their swinging,
our cats forgive us our logic and mediocrity —
that we sit on fastballs —
our dogs bark because it's their words exactly.

Our cats forgive us our logic and mediocrity,
they find us like seeing-eye singles.
Our dogs bark because it's their words exactly,
they couldn't have said it better themselves.

They find us like seeing-eye singles,
the announcers who tell us what to see.
We couldn't have said it better ourselves.
When you have a shadow behind the pitcher,

the announcers tell us what to see.
You'd see the white on the ball by that time.
You have shadows behind the pitcher
and everything looks dark.

You see the ball come out of his hand at that time,
but when it hits the shadows
it goes dark again
and you would whiff where it looks like it's moving exactly.

But when it hits the shadows
the traffic backs up.
You would whiff where it looks like it's moving exactly,
although the ball game is hard to watch on the radio.

Rational Parking

We can
only know
narratives

through past
events.

They shake us
into dis-
location

so we
can create
again,

the ends
of things
unpronounced.

Unpronounce-
able. Someone,
somewhere

is probably
overcooking,

is enveloping
your car,
will steer you.
It goes
without saying.

There's courage
there, but only
as a space

for the humor-
ous, a way
to talk back

or get
the last word

or visualize
space
before you

even start
the car.

II

A Simple Worker's Notebook

Special Prosecutor

For punishment is directed above all at others, at all the potentially guilty.

—Michel Foucault

I am riding in the passenger side of a rusted GeoPrism that once must have been the color of Tang. Kenneth Starr driving, obviously very much in love with me. He tries too hard, beams every time he looks up at me no matter what I'm saying. His smile strains across his face, threatens to open a gash below his nose and rip the flesh from his cheeks. He hands me a green canvas satchel he just bought. I am supposed to be impressed. The satchel resembles one I use for teaching — green, canvas, practical, compact. Mine cost $14.95 at the university bookstore, but the price tag on his is $872.00.

•

I'm not sure why he's taking us to Ohio, but I'm along for the ride. In the present moment. Deep listening.

•

This is very, very nice, I say, especially all these little pockets for pens & paper clips. Really, this is a fine bag. And look, you can put books in this compartment and they will be separate from papers, which you can put in this compartment.

He tilts his head toward me. Ken Starr's toothy smile. When he smiles, his wire-rimmed glasses reach for his arching forehead. He scans me for a glimpse of reciprocation, but I direct my eyes back to the road. The dashed center line is painted orange. He drives carefully despite his anxiety to please me.

•

Look here, I tell him. I found a strong, netted section — perfectly sized for documents — hanging in the middle of satchel, separated by two zippered compartments. I am a good listener, people-person, high emotional-intelligence quotient. Look at this, I say. Next time you take the President to court, you can put all your documents in this sack. What a nice bag you have here.

•

Always the firm handshake, I was taught, but don't grip too long. I unzip a side pocket and an enormous garment bag — complete with clothes hangers — inflated itself from the side of the satchel. The garment bag is geometrically impossible. No way the satchel could hold a secret compartment this size. And even so, why would it be secret?

Let others break eye contact first. It's the eyes, don't look at the lips. The eyes.

•

I can still remember Diane and Dave's place after all these years. An elegant sprawling gabled farmhouse. It anchors an acre of southern Ohio corn. It was too big for them so they kept boarders. We thought about starting a commune. They took good care of the place but couldn't keep the money straight from the boarders. They came to me with their problems and I listened. That's what people do, it's what you're supposed to do. Don't turn away your friends. If you can't be honest with them, then who are you trying to fool? Diane and Dave keep their arms around me as we walk through their empty living room. They want to stay close to me, and for some reason I speak in low tones fearing eavesdroppers. In that hush I tell them Ken Starr is staying at their boarding house and I need to get away. They say nothing, their silence a mystery I'm content to leave unsolved. Their arms around me, they escort me into the kitchen, a huge converted gymnasium with rows of picnic tables. Migrant laborers, mostly men but a few women, squished at every table eating eggs and toast heaped on every plate. It's clear to me that Diane and Dave's house serves as a way station, an underground railroad of sorts. A cell in a network of fake identities, citizenship papers, resettlement. I look down at the floor as we speak. If someone sees this, maybe my gaze, downward and focused, can make the conversation look casual. It's the secret force of well-being, it glides past obstacles in dreams and only perches, an unmoved sentry, when we're awake. *Everyone must see punishment not only as natural, but in his own interest; everyone must be able to read in it his own advantage.* The floor is tiled as if someone half-gutted and nearly rehabbed a turn-of-the-century tenement. I imagine whole families living in rooms with no privacy but for blankets draped in thresholds where doors should be. Diane and Dave keep their heads down, too, with faked ease, vigilance concealed, with business as usual. We'll watch his movements in the boarding house, we'll watch so he doesn't snuff out this settlement.

Oh, Death

1.
I cross the street
with a group of Americans.

We're the ones in shorts and sandals.
A man takes off black sunglasses,

a skirt swishes. Traffic police wear pumps.

A gypsy told me not to cross.
Feel this sheet pulling over me, he sang,

an old death song in a jar of coins.

2.
It's all right, I tell myself
you're just crossing

at the intersection of Houston and Elm
with an American debate club.

The debaters aren't afraid — they pursue clues.
Cars fade down the hill

huffing the Dallas pavement
to the triple underpass.

3.
In Rome the police wear expensive shoes,
direct traffic and wave long cigarettes.

In a recurring dream, I've lived there a year
without buying a ticket for the bus

and gotten away with it.
But I'm afraid to tell the driver

he missed my stop. The gypsy's in my ear —

I lock their jaws so they can't talk
stiffen their legs so they can't walk.

Close their eyes so they can't see —
This very air come and go with me —

4.
We go into the book depository.
Yellow tape around the boxes, in Texas

even gun nests are bounded — tender desert light
through the window against textbook boxes

all straw and nettles. I feel we shouldn't
be here, my wife and I on the sixth floor

on mousey school tiles.

5.
Sunlight runs up the grassy slope
toward the railway yards.

Feel this sheet pulling over me.

You think everything has its place
in Texas. The cabs stupefied

at the airport like cattle.

6.
A gypsy family gets too close but I shouldn't
shove the boy off the sidewalk.
I'm holding on to my pockets.
The harmonium player croons

Cast aside the flesh of thee, cast aside and set you free.
My wife asks him to stop.

Soldier, 1942

It's the first time he's knotted a tie.
In this standard flag-and-smile
boot camp headshot, Japan can be
just a wrinkle in the sky.
His girlfriend's father reads Italian newspapers
to the old men back in the neighborhood
who supported Mussolini
until we said he's the enemy.
Now they don't need newspapers.
Back on the farm
his younger brother and father build
the family's first flush toilet without him.
Back of the photo, he writes:
"Hey, ma & dad, this is supposed to be me."
Me, too, black-and-white patina, splinters,
I study his image as it crumbles
in my hands, like damp wood flaking from
the backyard tool shed we tore down
when I was 12.
          Well, he tore it down.
I carried planks away, nicked by their splinters.
They concealed themselves in the wood,
hiding until you gripped your hardest
then cut you. Age left its scratches
in the hasty stock background, gray scrim,
of this photograph. I'm tempted
to drop it, spare myself.
But the splinters chew my fingers convincingly,
his humble bluster, ready to take down Japan,
our ontology: this is supposed to be me.
My resistance, my disbelief in beginnings,
their power to name you, could be so much

heresy, or just something that burns
and goes away when sons believe in history.
I can almost see the roiled anatomy of Yalta
foretold in the sediment of this photograph,
in my father's eyes flush-brown
with maps and legends like he's asking the camera
what he'll see when he's shipped away.
He's enlisted, ready to fight.
He pretends war is curious, he'll keep secrets.
He'll take down a whole country, he'll partition
the world, just tell him where to go.

The Party Turns Fifty

Television is about people sitting in their living room
looking at their things.
                                    —Allen Ginsberg

One room
        across the river
                from Boston — a man, woman, their TV.

                Night spills too soon, morning
evening colder now, their summer fades.
        Behind baby blue blazer,
                Dan Rather picks each syllable

                like fish at market, red-eyed carp
left raw, washed clear in mounds of ice.
        No one listens here across the river from Boston —
                a man, woman, TV, blue light speechless.

                Dan Rather says, "The extravaganza in
Tiananmen was the climax of a day
        of highly organized activities."
                Plaster lips shape the words

                his frozen face has blushed,
each syllable melts ice cubes
        to footage, tanks belly-crawling
                Changan Avenue into the Square.

The man remembers
        that day two weeks past martial law
                they tanned body-to-body, soft ocean stones.

They met before the bloody common.
He almost stayed at home with his things
     alone, television clean — the news white china
       caught under glass over there.

      She tended bar weekends, days stuffed files
for Harvard Yenching Institute.
     They talked enough that night
       of martial law, visiting scholars,

      eyes skipped from peel
bottle wrappings to barroom TV.
     Two weeks later they scooped
       stone plains of sand in palms.

Now their TV, across the Charles,
     the fiftieth birthday of the revolution
       and they say no one really died June 4th.

     Dan's voice hoses blood
from stone until there's no such thing
     as history. He says, "Under the watchful eye
       of overhead windows, protestors voiced their anger

      toward Beijing." The screen breaks blue shadows
on their faces, September windows chill
     the backs of their necks. He touches her,
       a moment between two breaths or blinks:

      That which appears is good, she says,
and that which is good appears — and touches him back,
     secrets they finally understand,
       a box for all their things. Two chairs,

      two cups of tea, the television, Dan Rather:
"Fireworks in Tiananmen Square today,
     but only the festive kind." Half past the hour.
       Autumn air gnaws their ears, their living room

grows too cold. Breaths mingle,
with steam from their cups
        with blue chill from the screen
                then vanish inside the square of these four thin walls.

Smuggled Video

Head polished with cornices of snow.
Barrel neck huffed from crimson-yellow robes,

tough refugee skin splashed by varnish.
Calloused fingers press your lips in reflex

when troops scale your monastery.
You hold your tongue.

Falling monks flicker. Kickboots, bayonets,
light shards lulled from the TV monitor.

Voiceover traps the camera going,
tells us what we can imagine.

The People's Soldiers rolling monasteries.
Snake-line monks, nuns chanting in the street

soon arrested. This secret film jumps —
your blessing in Boston, hissing sand globes

mandalas shaped like doorways
to capture the body at rest.

Next cut too sharp — these secret images,
their impermissible dissolves and fades,

enough to make us dizzy.
Green soldiers remain, starched and posing

in their rubble, pretending to be narrators.

A Simple Worker's Notebook

I give my story, allow pictures. Later, story is distorted — sent without my permission, that is.

— Lee Harvey Oswald, "Historic Diary"

He's disappeared. His train arrives. He has tokens. He's not just another worker anymore. Newspapers blown, lost mail on platform. Nobody's clothes look much like his own. White shirt, black slacks he wore when he checked into the Hotel Metropole straight from Botkin Hospital. In the train station the cold swirl. Their heads down most of the time, he tries to look more or less like everyone. He wants a piece of this history.

He's a crack in the cement, lifeline tickling his palm. He planned so much he's left himself naked. Sees a blur in the corner of his eye. The huff of the train. The numbers don't add up. As soon as he puts them together he forgets them. Nothing counts, especially not delight, especially not here. He writes: *I amount to nothing in both systems.* He'll turn it upside-down, his precious diary, in order to read between the lines, shake himself from the caught-between pages. He looks at his watch, frowns on cue like any other commuter. Rush-hour trains never fast enough. He mimics. Rubs palm to forehead. The train is late, he'd like to say, but to speak this way would be like wearing someone else's clothes. His ventilated brow, briefcase, styrofoam coffee — he'll slip past them, invisible, the patsy countless once and for all. Twin headlights round the corner. Here it comes. The train is late.

Three months before he left for Minsk, he soaked his wrist in cold tap running numb against the knife, bled spiderwork into steaming tubwater. He wrote: *I thought, When Rimma comes at 8 to find me dead it will be a great shock.* He's disappeared. He tries to laugh at

himself. Some days he's infectious. Or he's a paper clip keeping
a page inside a shaken spine. Or just scrap paper marking private
lives unread in his diary. He counts on it, clasped to his chest, his
secret history, a simple worker's notebook. Trains slow, running
on holiday schedule, the platform receding in backdraft.

On the freighter back to America, he wouldn't let Marina on deck
because he was ashamed of her clothing. She trusted him. They'll
be countless, cold stars, he said. He told her to let him handle
everything. They're not petty officials — he had plans. He held
a rifle in the backyard in Dallas. A copy of *The Militant* fanned
in front of him like he was some kind of geisha. That night he
saw lights in the sky, not constellations. He saw prime numbers
and they were historical.

Fever of Unknown Origin

He does the crossword with a shot of whiskey.
        Every morning under the tree he planted when
his daughter was born. Watches his neighbors get into cars
        with coffee mugs and lunch bags. He's retired from it.
If you ask, he'll tell you he guarded German POWs, the occasional G.I.
        who got drunk and crashed a jeep. He tells you he's over
the Japanese, it's been too many years. He can't sleep

in his bed because his hands go numb. Afraid his daughter
        will move in with him if the kid becomes a hobo.
Turned half his backyard into a garden, gives away zucchini
        to his golf buddies. He kept most of the sedatives
Doc prescribed when the kid made off with his car, crashed it
        drunk into a ditch — her divorce. He took a couple,
broken in half with a murky fingernail, but didn't need them
        after that. They made his eyes heavy, like his body took a bribe.
Can't sleep a full night, not enough to dream — his naps forgettable,
        pragmatic. Often wakes himself just to put his watch
next to the coffeemaker so he'll remember it tomorrow.

Heat rises. Here's a man in sweater and ball cap chilled in August
        in his living room. Doctors call it fever of unknown origin:
101 degrees or more, at least three weeks of it, and your physician
        must be baffled. Doc tells him they go away on their own,
these fevers. He imagines them as beginningless, a shift in the wind,
        gale in your face when it seemed to prop your back.
Keeps tiny pills. In the cabinet, beneath the kitchen wall clock,
        useful, patient, like the big sycamore peeling in the backyard,
outliving the family who planted it.

Autoresponder@whitehouse.gov

Thank you for writing
to President Clinton via electronic mail.
Since June 1993,
       tactics include unexpected shining
              of a flashlight in a victim's face, intermittent
                awakenings
the President has received
over 2.3 million messages from people across the country
and around the world. Online communication
has become a tool
       for observation, tying victims hands behind their backs
            so that they cannot cover their faces.
                Around-the-clock scrutiny
to bring government
and the people closer together.
Because so many of you write, the President cannot
personally review each message, though he does
receive samples
       and intrusive face-to-face interrogation
of his incoming correspondence.
The White House Correspondence staff helps him read
and respond to the mail.
       Individuals being tortured are usually physically
            isolated or else made to feel isolated.
All responses are mailed via U.S. Postal Service.
This is the only electronic message
you will receive from *whitehouse.gov*,
       as torture destroys an individual's sense of
            personal control.

No other message purporting to be from the President or his staff
with address at *whitehouse.gov* is authentic —
       the physical logistics
                of questioning torture survivors
                      recapitulates psychologically the torture and
                      isolation.
       If you have received such a message,
you have received a "spoof."
We appreciate your interest in the work of the Administration.
The taken-for-granted expectation of eye contact
                is an almost impossible task for the torture survivor.

State of the Union

With a bridge and tunnel to Canada, a long open lakefront, the largest concentration of Arab-Americans in the United States, the regional supply of fresh water, and a nuclear reactor just down the road, there is plenty to worry about here.

—Jodi Wilgoren, THE NEW YORK TIMES

Valerie came because she is concerned. Because anything can come in the mail. She'll watch out. It's all inconvenient. Senator Levin's

a little embarrassed by the attention. He summed up domestic security as three C's. Common Sense. Confidence. And Community.

Colonel Sturdivant used three P's. Planning. Preparedness. Proactive. A sign was posted on the door, listing prohibited items:

posters, flatware, handcuffs, drugs, aerosols, ammunition, or "weapons-like objects (bats, clubs, batons, etc., including toys

and replicas)." The Police Department's new Mobile Field Force, in military pants and gas masks, paraded on stage,

followed by a firefighter in hazmat suit who looked, wrapped in tinfoil, like an awkward giant. Duct tape and plastic sheeting were less important

than blankets and batteries. *If I were scared, I'd be at home in a closet*, Valerie said. *This is "concerned." I just want to know enough*

to be knowledgeable. Two dozen neighborhood watch-captains and radio patrollers clutched a color-coded sheet for what to do:

"A High Condition (Orange) is declared when there is a high risk. Prepare to execute contingency procedures." Because of orange.

There is plenty to worry about here. It's all inconvenient.
It can come at any time. Things arrive, then you do

something about them. It's all very terrifying.

It Came from a Clarinet

He flinched and paid for it.
Came back from touring
with Stracchini's Big Band,
found babies every time,
eight kids, four miscarriages.
He raised a farm from two acres
of patch and sump,
brought coal buckets with him
when he cut trees for the house.
He taught each son on clarinet.
The breath, hollow,
tapers into crystal,
and the trick, he said,
you call this *melody*. You make it
sound like it's coming
from diamond fingertips,
from reed, chime,
not your pink and dirty lungs.

·

When he leaned his ear
to his friends' mouths,
he seemed too young
to be going deaf.
His ear oily, aging at 24.
They didn't know whether to speak
louder or take a bite from it.

·

Historians say Benny Goodman
practiced hours every day
until he died. He traced spirals
in the air with his clarinet,
his body blowing, a screen door
flapping the wind.
Between songs, he was lost,
clarinet cradled in his arms.

•

The ship, *Taormina*, he took
to America sunk four years later
by German torpedo.
When he closes his eyes
he hears the *padrone*
walking the deck. He waves
sheet music so he'll be left alone.
He has jobs waiting, he'll be useful.
The *padrone* never touched him.

•

It came from a clarinet,
from the basement a piece
of an old Italian song
no one could remember anymore.

•

Benny Goodman said to Artie Shaw,
"This thing will never let you down,"
which, for Shaw, was a strange thing
to say about a piece of wood
with some keys on it. For Artie,
"Jazz was born in a whiskey barrel."

•

It was like composing.
The patriarch of the basement
played out his memories on piano
before writing them down,
in an alcove with an echo
where they stacked sheet music.
His hands still burning
from the brass factory,
his ears clotted with grease,
those fingers moved
up and down the clarinet like mice
running in the walls.

Back to the Farm, 12/7

War was on when Frank and Rose
came back from a nickel movie.

He touched her hand, she gripped
back so hard he lost his breath.

Rows of green peppers in mud
coughed back to the wind.

They kissed at the fencepost, where
he carved "1928" as a little kid.

His brothers would tend to planting.
They talked of marriage, but maybe

it was just a lot of polished words,
amplified G.I. sepiatones and rows

of metal bunks in spitwax floors
in their letters, V-mail from England.

Frank called her "loving wife," Rose played
back, "dear husband." He shined his shoes

the color of eggplant, his uniform drab.
Beans just poked from the dirt,

tasty enough for rabbits to eat. He posed
for her with his rifle, sent his parents

a portrait in schoolboy eyes, crooked tie,
waiting to grow into his uniform.

Two shoulder arrows for Private, an army
police whistle hanging from a uniform pocket.

Tip of steel-cover Bible nudged from
other pocket, to keep away bullets they say.

Picture for Rose his Sunday starch whites,
M-1 pointing off the frame, eyes cocked

as if peeping at a rabbit, frozen,
twitching at the start of a bean.

III

Thinking While Held Down

Bibles for Vietnam

He talks like he's nibbling pistachios,
winces through reconstructed cheeks.

He found God when he jumped in a pond
and the fire wouldn't stop.

He's the one who got me, the vet
whose phosphorous grenade went off in his hand

in windup at Bien Hao. He tells Jim
what "phosphorous" means to soldiers

on fire, the flames even burn through water.
You look long enough at the sun, he says,

you realize it's fire in the sky, got as much right
to be there as a sunflower, that's the scary part.

His face, a mask of surgeries, you'd think
it's cut by acne if you didn't know,

like my brother, who came back
with pimple scars and memories of surveillance trails

and a Samsung camera he bought me in Saigon.
Jim's listening, it's easy, as simple

as Sunday morning newspaper and coffee.
Give the Vet some money, Bibles for Vietnam.

We watched these testimonies before school
each morning, my mother and I,

a young boy growing out of my own ribs,
away from her, quiet, clever.

She pledged by phone to Jim Bakker's
theme park, out there, the kitchen.

For the first time, I understood the things
you're warned against are the ones

you're best suited to accomplish.
A spirit must have taken over: a mare, goblin,

Black Madonna, Italian rustic
voodoo of her girlhood, the old country.

Almost silent, the dark and easeful slide
of a confessional door, PTL each morning

a wafer in my palms until I couldn't talk
to her anymore.

The Vet wiggled, he won't be comfortable
in chairs the rest of his life. He's here

for food and Bibles. No, for Thailand.
That's right, Vietnam's next, he says,

once they let Americans back in.
Before I understood the colonial missionary,

or monks pitched forward,
matchsticks in the street,

I assumed he was one of us, I was one of them.
Cross-purposed Protestant or Catholic all the same,

taking it like we deserved it, the kind of fire
that burns right through water.

Jim Bakker, chimp-faced barker
bestowed upon us, coming by the magic

of satellite TV, brand-new,
a pastor who doesn't drink wine

bare his teeth or belch at mass.
We all come out from trailers, even Jim,

but some of us build amusement parks
and talk with satellites in the sky.

In quiet his confessional slid open,
a priest's head in the shadows,

Jim Bakker's gelatinous body.
I found her secret. She gave to his theme park,

committed us in monthly payments,
clandestine phone calls from the kitchen

when Tammy Faye sang "We're Blessed"
at the end of every broadcast.

Thinking While Held Down

—*after Jenny Holzer*

She wrote her last check at 10:30 to Mellon Bank, their two-hundred dollar car loan. Then she flickered. Bird's wings, her head, not like lift or glide but the wings themselves. Her living room split into blood hemispheres, one side stunned in rip-current, the other overwhelmed. It must have become predatory, her living room, the carpet weave, the VCR, the ceiling light fixtures they special-ordered in 1962 shaped like diamonds. She would've told her husband this, thinking it while held down, a mother with no real power.

Nurses comb her so she doesn't shrink any deeper into her shoes. At home we find a stack of clothes and rags in the hamper, her insurance policies at the bottom waiting all these years for us like a pulsar sits patiently for a deep space camera to find its steady blinking comfort. Today I taught my father to pay his first bills since 1956. We touched my mother's mathematics, her rage for balance. We pretended it made her laugh, a shy sliver moon peeking through a breeze of stars, it was so dark. We tracked her checkbook ledger, matched it with receipts. My father stopped when we found the check for Mellon Bank. He knew it was 10:30 because *Matlock* was half-over, fixed himself a sandwich and half-shot of Amaretto every day when it started.

He took a bite, he thinks, when she moaned, it whisked out of her like nothing he heard in 43 years of marriage. He remembers, past the table in the kitchen, checkbook and stacks of bills, until he sees her now, sitting, the couch and her carpet weave, VCR, her mouth moving up and down. Her stroke, those two bitter diamond ceiling fixtures now turned out of their skins in nonsense, her Lascaux tomb no one will find for 17,000 years.

Visiting Hour

1.
Their shoes too big, they shift in them.
Sometimes you think they're balanced
on their arches, their feet bottoms gone fleshy
like the dull sky through the window
above the thermostat.
They shift in shoes worn from pacing,
deliver themselves body and bone,
sun shafts cast in dust.

2.
Stink of mashed potatoes rises
from your tissues, they tolerate your bed,
its zoo fence rails for leaning on you.
You sweat sheets, a chain-linked rosary,
stiff-collared angels. Their priest cups
your hands in his professional palms.

3.
Words gather their sleepless mounds,
it's their language now,
gibberish smudges your face.
After dinner, alone, God's hawk wings
span your bed but don't stay long
enough. The shadow leaves
its fur in splotches on your eyes,
skin November cool with dew,
body vulnerable as butter. It's quiet again.
The room is hatching, listen,
a steady wind throbs against the window.

The Dead So Tired Watching

You dead must be eight feet tall
when we let you out.
You want to reach, pick us up
when we stumble over
children's toys on the carpet.
You're obligated to show
some concern for us,
the tired living, too busy
to keep our dream journals
and frustrated we can't
remember them in the morning.
You don't understand
the groggy salt bouquet I pinch
over my shoulder to keep
you at arm's length.
We can feel you watching.

You don't touch us.

We can make it back ourselves.
We don't need to remember
those dreams where you return
and sit so high in the recliner chair
tired from looking after us.
You, the mother whose dead parents
crouched in your hospital room,
the black tomcat who jumped
on impulse from a moving car,
the boy spilled with his canoe
and sunk. Tired from watching.
Your fringe grin at dawn
along the reeds when you see

new stalks grown overnight.
To us, it's just a swamp,
languid and pecked by crows,
our eyes fixed forward,
floating in their murk.
Your hands steady each rich,
nameless step, as if waving
pedestrians through the crosswalk.

Corrosive

Sand ripples from her shoes.
Her years of borders cannot
exceed this swell, urge of sea
she came for, poised between
spark and plunge, a mother
concealed by earth and tide.
We could baptize you
just like when my family came.
Except just your feet.
Glass mountains erased
in watercolor, cliff house
sliced into sand. She knows
other voices, too, they crack
the lock of your door,
burn your mouth in prayer.
You look down, then away
as he passes. And never look back
at yourself, the space behind
your navel scorched.
Etches close to surf,
each foamy lift, wave,
chased by sea that spawned it:
mother, father back in their old country
as if they never left at all.
She comes for them now,
a child raised, a globule
in the churn, an unlocked
cell built into rock.
She thinks again: *We could baptize you.*
Except just your feet. Bends to laces
gnarled nine hours by airports.
Frees a stubborn knot, the grayest wave

tonight drapes her feet.
Bare, she is the Black Madonna
of her family, where blessed lambs,
dumb offerings, still burn
for her in charcoal, for harvest.
The ocean stings, this ache
her mother's witchcraft,
these drowning rocks.
This high tide corrodes the sand.

Giuseppina's Stone

Walking still, she ordered
back in '63 granite dusk,
starlight speckle. Seemed

treasure really, toothy splint
making time. Mother somehow
knew in marble grass to find

stones each birthday,
holiday. Till sure Grandma
next to husband would bury

her slowing body, retract
the lope from waiting.
Testimony of endings,

eighteen years her empty spot,
its wasting. She breathed grooves
in that rock. Stones do not

change, but a half-filled plot
marks her last year in rock.
Her name into that hole.

Face on Mars

Play of light and shadow in the Cydonia region snapped
by Viking Orbiter, a forehead slopes carved

in millennia of wind and gravity. A trick —
the lonely face of distance,

a prisoner's solitary hallucination.
Tonight: the Leonid meteor shower, debris

only visible in the Midwest this week. Streaks,
I make them wiggle into fireworks, anxious green,

another trick of the eyes. A secret mirror,
that sense of collusion between seer and seen.

I used to stare at the back of heads to make
them itch. I look hard enough to make it real, learn it takes

the gaze of ancient astronauts, or the last look
a mother gives before she reaches for her pills.

I followed her smoke helix, Salem filters,
rise from the ashtray while my father fell

dead on the couch — overtime at the mill.
When I look at my family, I see the Face on Mars

staring back. Eyes dumb as streetlights, two pearl sacks
beat-up from memory, I cross North Avenue. Green tails

streak west to east. Someone sneaks a handicapped spot
at Kinko's, other cars roll past,

discordant as space junk. In Cydonia,
mute mesas and buttes, a scattering of ruins,

monumental enough. Stares back till one of us blinks.

IV

The Lama's English Lessons

The Day We Talk About Imaginary Numbers

I'll tell you I stare at trees
But I don't classify them.
You'll say you do,
We'll explain it with numbers —

You'll ask
What part of the equation
I'd like to be.

I'll say I want
To nest in a bouquet
Of parentheses,
To be the microcosm
That needs to be solved
Before you can go further.

That's how people
React to you anyway, you'll say.

I'll never tell
When I see you
As a plus-minus sign
Sitting cross-legged
In the branches of a tree
I can't name.

I'll be there
Watching you glide
In a beautiful
Asymptote,
Infinitely closer
Toward an x axis
You never intend to touch.

The Body is Fragile

A gull flicks down on a wave,
flies back against cutting wind into fog.

He clipped a speck between his claws,
an impossible fish, an inkspot pulled from the sea,

a new story, our memories cresting,
fresh mouths playing with our food.

Follow me back to a time when I didn't know
the body is fragile. Try to make it fresh,

like it's our first time over and over again.
I try to remember it for you,

the straight look of nothing special
about to happen, if you could remember

what the Cuyahoga looked like before it burned.
A whole city shuddered, scorched by its own river.

I recall, for you, my last breath before
the whoosh of baseball bat — that flash I remember,

too young to know why I couldn't exhale.
At tables around us, no one notices me

telling this story from so long ago,
when another kid smacked me with a bat

from behind, a gust of air that sent me
reeling. You taste a little garlic and anise

in the last knocky frames of free fall.
Sure, like your pasta plate right now,

this is how the brain abandons, strips you
for the two-bit thuggery and bare bulb

of the senses. That blow flared me, numb,
the field I fell rippled in front of me,

danced in blown branches. Everything went black,
but that's cliché and you say we can do better.

Old lovers, let's make it come alive — the napkins
on our laps, a wine bottle, the other tables snooping

for the bat crack — real groundswell and tide,
my young knees soft as tennis balls.

My Vertigo

As if from a drum machine. Quarter-note pulses.
　　　I hear a tick-tock in the middle
of my head. I'm dizzy when I get up or turn around.
　　　This is not a poetry trick. My sloppy head
is not some symbol of something else. I'm dizzy.
　　　I'm scheduled for an appointment with Dr. Purcell
tomorrow, but till then I'm awash every time
　　　I stand up, turn my head. Might as well be a man
built to swing with skyscraper winds.
　　　Shelly says check the new age web sites, maybe
my chakras are opening. The same thing
　　　happened five years ago. Dr. Engleman said it wasn't
stroke, heart valve, brain tumor, or diabetes.

　　　She said it goes away, that the medicine prescribed
for this malady actually stands you up
　　　in a small raft, the water green and the sky slate with storm,
before it makes you better. Sounded like leeches,
　　　or cold baths for fever, so I figure I'll take my chances
with chakras — those quarter-notes struck
　　　by drum machine programmers who pull the song down
so low, tell their lies so well about the spur of the moment
　　　that our watches sputter and no one
leaves the room without dancing.

　　　When I was 16, I learned the word "vertigo"
a week into the hospital with dizzy spells.
　　　I tested it with my nurse: *The room spins when I get up —*
it's vertigo. She nodded, helped me into
　　　a wheelchair. Dr. Kirkland said it was bacteria
in my urine. I was afraid of him, so I couldn't say
　　　they actually started the night I dreamed my grandmother,

just two weeks dead, climbed into a carriage
        pulled by Emily Dickinson's horses and gestured with
her shaky hand I come with her. I was sinking
        into my bed, down down down down, and dizzy.

Fat

Witnesses should have seen the two of them.
As he lost his breath halfway up the stairs
she said it: *You're so fat. Can't you
move any faster?* He turned around,
smiled so wide he squinted, told her
he walked fast as he could. *I know*, she said,
clever for a fifth-grader, *Move faster, Lard Ass.*
He memorized patterns, grids from
each stair, told her, *Take it back*,
back where a fat boy stares down a ceiling
to fall asleep. He draws those blocks tonight,
pointer finger traces each axis in the dark.
Behind his plodding, her chubby stomach crept
the blue edges of her skirt. Breathless
from these steps, he reached the top.
He wanted to say they made gym clothes
only for skinny kids who can do situps,
do a hundred, but her gray and white pinstripes
hit that top stair and nothing made sense, his heaving,
her swell, unfit for hallways filled with healthy kids.
The other bodies filed past his shape,
tits they told him he was growing.
Other kids blew a circle around them,
so she told him, Lard Ass, to turn around.
He pushed her against the green-tiled wall,
perfect squares in graph-papered porcelain,
held her with left hand, drew right fist behind his neck.
Told her take it back, watched steel-blue eyes turn
burred metallic then gray. Three of them stopped,
urged him to belt her — they would go down together,
fist pulled back, all eyes drawn around
the two of them — if he hits, she shuts up

maybe they stop if he hits her.
Witnesses should have seen the two of them,
how the kids pushed, walked past
as if those two were dusty textbooks.
The other fat kids, even the diabetic,
looked straight ahead that second, fist pulled back.
He saw some shared secret in their misfit clothes,
a hidden curse, spraddled wires, a history
waiting to be cut. By now the kids were bored.
He felt alive for once, those few seconds he decided.
She'll be his first girlfriend, his next — knuckle pop
to skin never stops, no matter the weight they lose.
Fingers pinch wires, too tight to snap, their history
shared, strung up. That second deciding, fist pulled
back, all stare back as if those two were children.

Evidence

This is discovery. It's evidence
of our big brains at work,
like the liability waiver we sign
about cougars before they let us hike.
At 8,000 feet, I'm forced to bend over.
Hands on knees, heart punching
my chest. These are places where,
in the dark, I trust the country road
ends somewhere, clean air to kill for.

Everything we do without permission
feels like theft: three small logs,
ash at the center of a triangle.
Someone etched a fire pit at the top
of the hill, a secret I've stumbled on.
It's property. Killer bees and snakes live here.
A rainshower of stars, night sky
soaked in light. Something postures far away
in the trees, just the wind hauling itself
in high altitude. There are shadows here, of course.
Unlike me, they're not afraid
to come back from the edge of the world
with not a thing to show for it.

The Train from San Mateo

wants to speak,
probes for boundaries,
for horizon, until

the right words
find a seam.
The hills listen,

stubbled, a fine
fuzz, patient like
hairs on the

back of fingers.
Hills arch, hearts
still as reptiles.

Gimp scrubs wince
at the sun.
It says, "I'm

sticking with you,"
as if these
are the only

words it knows,
all trains lost
in that sweet,

lovesick spot in
your chest where
you can't see

the mirror wink,
and the shrug
of its loping

shoulders makes no
sense to you
anymore.

Palmistry

Your line is a vapor trail
that dissipates at the wrist.
That line's irreducible.
There's some dismal longitude,
but don't take yourself seriously.
Look for the radiance
of one-dollar toothbrushes.
You can tease a future
out of them but they have no nerve.
Fork at the wrist says
you're in danger of becoming
an object of suspicion
and ridicule over something
you may have gossiped about.
At this cross, you're someone
who wants to gain distinction
through his hard work.
You're the type of dreamer
who goes to a new city
and looks up your name
in the phone book.
But be careful if you forget
your name and don't know
whether to search
under "city" or "phone" or "self."
In dreams, to see one palm tree
standing alone is an omen
of the loss of a good friend.
You dream of rooms, big ones,
secret spaces, doors entered
from sunken living rooms
into play-spaces, decked out

suburban basements.
Nobody's been here before.
There should be plastic on the couch.
Houses of course are the body
inscribed with secret panels.
Plastic clenched along the floor,
empty-handed. It's been here for years
waiting like a castaway.

They Sound Bells For Us

Our cat sits on the windowsill like an old man
in shirtsleeves. She's arranging flowerpots.
When it rains, she hides under
the bed. My goddaughter is fighting
for custody of her child because her
boyfriend drinks and gambles his paycheck
from the plastic factory. Our families need
to visit us each summer to get away from
their troubles — to lock themselves in a room,
but there's nothing on TV then, anyway,
because it's summer and just as easy they can
get the Wisdom Channel on cable back home.
Our animals know when it's about to rain
and they hide underneath the easy chair
when a tornado's coming. Our friends
are nervous when you take pictures of cattle
grazing outside the Secretary of Defense's
winter home in Taos, a Chevy Chevelle rusted
and on blocks in the yard next door. It's
the times we live in. Don't worry, you
tell them, the cattle are running away and
the cameras in the Secretary's bird feeder
can document this. Like anyone, he is shaped
by childhood events: a memorable year in 1948,
for example, at a Boy Scout ranch outside Taos.
He keeps horses, a donkey, a mule, cats,
and a dachshund named Reggie. Our animals
will not let us bring them into the basement
when the air turns green and the sky purple.
If we move the easy chair, they'll just hide
somewhere else. We have to realize we cannot
protect them, even though we feed them, clean

their shit, hold them on the vet's polished metal
exam table. They know the smell of pollen
through our screens is not a sign of happiness,
or that the flight of a dove does not
symbolize peace, or clapper bells, or magisterial
silence. They can't even tell us if wings symbolize
only themselves. So how can we hope to protect
them or anyone? Even if, God forbid, a Pope
was demented, infallibility would still be present.
The Holy Spirit would stop him from saying
something like, "Jesus is really Mickey Mouse."
Bells are ringing. No one can see the white smoke,
so they sound bells for us.

Three Fresh Shelves, Left Wall of the Garage

First thing you see in this garage.
Forty-five bowls of clear plastic
on each shelf, shaped with paling hands,
palms calloused by the slow wear,
silence. Three shelves, a regiment,
a hundred thirty-five bowls testify:
beyond our genius we build
for what we plan to place on shelves.

But you cannot ask why until you really
see them — forty-five bowls of clear plastic
on each shelf. Nails, corks, screws,
oil, pencils, vaseline in each.
In case you cannot take them all
at one view, each is streaked with silver labels,
masking tape thick with magic marker signs
painted across, all capitals denoting
the object inside. His granddaughter
finds her crayons here, batteries there,
knows where to look for pencils,
lines of each letter soldered together
as if to front an architect's schematic.
He shows them off to his son, the poet,
a testament to stanzas, how they hold
their lines together like his corks,
saved in bowls marked *corks*,
plug errant jugs of coolant for the car.
From splattered years of linotype
he learned hieroglyphs do not aspire

to script, so his standards rise like birds
each morning.

Closer look, uniform bowls
seem unnatural — roundness withers
atop each rim like aging shingles
curled on the sun, the sharp plastic opaque
from dry fingertips, patient wear.
He holds each shape together
at the top with clumsy rings of leather
that once sheathed paper-cut saw blades.
From warped plastic — and this need
for leather — you see these never began
as dutiful bowls. Someone taught him
the shape of this desire, the need
to tell his granddaughter just where
she must park her bike for room for cars,
where to put her things, or where to find them.
She mixed double-A batteries in bowls
for triple-A. Her translation
stalks each stroke, his capital letters.

These are two-liter soda bottles
made into bowls by lamplight in his garage.
His hand glides a few long strokes of blade,
fixes a straight line for the top
of his plastic bowl. He stretches
the black plastic base away from the soda bottle
until he forces it flat, and the hard bottom
of the bottle drips a circular base, as if a vessel.
A garage is a shrine to our experience,
a house for making verse, where you hide food
for granddaughters who take it
as an embrace.

Closer, you see a paper plate of shrimp
for voodoo, a *minyan* in the mud,
or a Buddha made from twigs and dung.
Come in a few more steps, you see them

alphabetically, tracked by what they hold:
corks, drills, keys, lids, plastic caps, vaseline,
more than you can see from just one
quick sweep across the wall. We owe him
a closer look, the objects as he saw them,
the point he felt his breath tickle
his upper lip: corks spill like rocks
from their leather top; rusted drill bits
endure a bowl marked *drills*;
keys and lids and caps await assignment;
a new jar of vaseline inside the bowl
labeled *vaseline.*

The Lama's English Lessons

It's a language problem,
your head thrown
back, laughing.
In your new English,
you point
at the teapot
to offer me a cup.

You say I should
worry about tigers
lurking the kitchen,
        that you fixed
a "busted" egg
at breakfast.

No tigers in Cambridge.
I knew a dreamy
twenty-pound housecat,
dead ringer
for a mountain lion
videotaped
on TV news
        yeti yawning in
the White Mountains.
And, I say, we "break"
an egg to "fix" it
with morning coffee.

You repeat "fix"
and "worry."
I show you where
the tongue goes,

restrained muscle,
        how to draw
the mouth wide
for "fix,"
tight for "worry."

One finger frets
your lips,
in the other hand
you swarm
a line of rosary,
as if I missed,
brief and passing,
        the tiger
amazed
in the kitchen.

Notes

"Five Verses for Shariputra Mugged Outside His Building" is inspired by the story of the Buddha's disciple Shariputra, whose crisis of faith is recounted in *The Way of the Bodhisattva* (Padmakara Translation Group; Boston: Shambhala, 1997).

"Grace Notes" is for Chris George and Eric Krauter. The epigraph is from George Oppen's "Blood from the Stone."

"Rational Parking": Thanks to Tim Prchal for asking me to write a poem for this title.

"Special Prosecutor": The epigraph is from Michel Foucault's *Discipline and Punish*. The final section of the poem also adapts a line from Foucault's book.

"Oh, Death": The quotations are from two different versions of the song performed by Doc Boggs and Camper Van Beethoven.

"Smuggled Video" and "The Lama's English Lessons" are for Geshe Tsultrim Chöpel. "Smuggled Video" adapts a line from Alex Gildzen's "Allison."

"The Party Turns Fifty": The epigraph is from Allen Ginsberg's "Is About." The poem also adapts a quotation from Guy Debord's *The Society of the Spectacle*.

"A Simple Worker's Notebook" uses quotations from "Historic Diary," the journal that Lee Harvey Oswald kept from 1959-1962 in the Soviet Union.

"Autoresponder@whitehouse.gov" combines text from a White House autoresponder email form letter with a manual for counselors written by the Marjorie Kovler Center for the Treatment of Survivors of Torture.

Three Candles Press Titles

Digerati: 20 Contemporary Poets in the Virtual World
ISBN: 0-9770892-2-3, $15.95

RJ McCaffery, *Ice Sculpture of Mermaid With Cigar*
ISBN: 0-9770892-0-7, $12.95

Tony Trigilio, *The Lama's English Lessons*
ISBN: 0-9770892-1-5, $12.95

Available from Ingram, Amazon.com, Barnes & Noble, and through the press.

www.threecandlespress.com

Printed in the United States
87449LV00014B/229-246/A